# longing for life

rly

NEWMAN SPRINGS PUBLISHING
320 Broad Street
Red Bank, NJ 07701

First originally published by Newman Springs Publishing 2021

ISBN 978-1-63692-758-9 (Paperback)
ISBN 978-1-63692-759-6 (Digital)

Printed in the United States of America

to everyone i've loved & lost

# Contents

# life

my life was a redundant game of
ring-around-the-ros(ie):
the introvert,
surrounded by extroverts.

there i stood—always present
but never included.

playful but never quite fun.

—*the lonesome rose*

my advice,
take the scenic route
while you wander through
your life, my darling.

it's all about perspective
& since the moment i looked into my past,
i feel like i've been given hope for my future.

*—sense of tranquility*

we have been one
since before i knew how to claim things.

you were given to me.
unwrapped and willing to allow me
the ability to watch you grow
in front of my eyes
alongside me.

each and every year around the sun
watching our personalities unfold,
cheering for the countless
beautiful moments,
& providing utmost comfort
during terrible times.

without hesitation or
the slightest realization,
we made the choice
to stay together through and through

this is my favorite love story;
the strongest of bonds
proof that forever exists and that
love can be eternal in sisterhood and friendship.

—*my first friend*

to my favorite human:

thank you for always making me laugh
when i want to cry the most.

we don't need words with each other;
we simply know.

the world can disagree with us
& we will remain on each other's side.

our morbidity feels a little less cold
when we are cozy together.

i will celebrate you until the end of time;
we are timeless.

nothing can touch this bond.

there is nothing i wouldn't do for you.
you are made of the most incredible things.
i wish for you to always see you as i see you.

i never understood how you put up with me, but you
always claim there are no flaws to be seen.

so i've realized that
i am your reflection.
you bring me back to myself every time.

*−lucky to love you*

my native tongue has taught me to
understand genius, love, and joy.

a hereditarily hard exterior that aided the molding of the
mind.

cyrillic worked as a window to delve into cultural nuances,
respect for diversity,
& oh-so-many superstitions.

proud to be culturally me.

clothing worn
music listened to
& traditions practiced
can become an off-putting aesthetic
to those who judge and cannot relate.


—*culture shock*

my family escaped a dictatorship
only to dictate everything i do;
some things you just can't unlearn...

*—the oppressed murmured to the oppressor*

i derive from a family of
immigrants and criminals.
left to my own devices by
parents who couldn't parent

"teaching" me that it can be better to
go through life unnoticed.

to remember that emotions can be a weakness
to always protect my mind, body, and soul.

i entirely owe and blame
what i've become
on that,
on them.

*—upbringing*

how can my kindness
be mistaken for weakness
if i was never kind?

i am not made for weakness;
i was raised to be
strong.

so strong that
i will break you down
just to prove i'm built better.

pent up adolescent angst smolders
through my veins as i puff out my chest
& lock my knees to prove they will not buckle.

i will never allow myself to be weak,
so, does that make me strong?

i'm still deciding...

my childhood home housed me for over twelve years.

my childhood home kept a roof over my head regardless of whether we could afford to pay the bills.

my childhood home held the opportunity for lessons to be learned.
they were insightful yet undetected.

my childhood home was soundproof enough for the neighbors not to hear my screams.
it was able to insulate my pain.

my childhood home was a place i constantly ran from in hopes to not be dragged back.
i never stood a chance.

my childhood home did not leave me with much of a childhood at all.

*—searching for sanctuary*

her red lips
held together by a fine slit line;
lips that once seemed inviting.

take a closer look...
once opened, they released venom
sewn together
with words of deceit.

*—where my trauma was born*

i spit bullets,
without ever contemplating
the exit wounds.

brandishing insults,
armed just the same as my shrill mother's mouth.

they say a child does learn by example...

*—lessons from red lips*

it has been said that
*"every rose has its' thorn."*

i ponder my thorns as i attempt to remove
the stiletto-stained scar
my mother dug into
the stem
of my spine.
at the ripe age of nine.

french
is usually used in terms of romance.

if that were the case,
then the painted fingernails
my mother slapped me with
left me
lovestruck.

"get out, you were never my daughter. i never loved you!"

those words
ten sharp-painful words

were said so calmly yet cutthroat,
engulfed with heavy hatred.

they hit me like a ton of bricks.

*—a mother's final words*

i came to expect her quick movements in attempt to prepare for the moments when she struck me.

still i was caught off guard, struck with surprise, when she rapidly emptied the house and allowed it to stay vacant.

—her exit

can't keep feeling lost
without knowing
what's next,
where,
& on what day.

i've always been bad with directions.
so, pardon me, will you please help me?

don't leave me here alone
because if it wasn't abundantly clear,
i suffer from abandonment already
all on my own.

"how is it possible for a mother to detest and abandon her own child? it doesn't make any sense!"

they say to me
with empathetic tones
& shell-shocked eyes.

nevertheless,
here i stand,

living
breathing
proof that there is an exception
to every rule.

maslow's monkeys have nothing on me.
"you cannot choose your family,"
is what they say.

i say, who the fuck are "they" anyway?
i suppose in the most literal of form, it is verifiable.

you cannot choose your family,
although,
my family chose to dispose of me.

what does that tell you?
what does that make me?

−*black sheep*

i made sure i excelled at all the things my mother said i couldn't do.

an arguably ethical juxtaposition.

i forced myself to focus on
becoming a better and brighter me
in spite of her.

*—i learned from pain*

my father always wanted a daughter
but wasn't ready to raise one.

growing up, i was always surrounded by care
but never with a woman's touch.

toy dolls turned into toy trucks.

pink always seemed to be blue.

so i became the best son a daughter could be...

—*masculine me*

would you love me even if i wasn't yours?

*—paternity test aside*

my father is an utter mess
who always tries his best even with
tequila coating the inside of his chest.

born with a motherly instinct
that not many men possess.

he seamlessly surpassed
the capabilities of a woman
& effortlessly took on both parental roles.

he never allowed me to feel the absence of the one who
left by being a mother in her stead

until michelle was able to help him bear
the burden that was me as a teen.

i am so lucky to be able to call him my parent;
to share his dna.

hoping to make him proud
as the last line of lineage.

the family name lives on in me.

you always told me
if i had one good friend in my life,
i was lucky,

& it turns out
i'm the luckiest
because that one friend is you.
the one who made me, me.

—папина дочка
*(daddy's girl)*

i majored in the art of indecisiveness.
one of the first lessons was that life is all a test,
& i hoped that if i worked hard enough, i'd pass.

most of my life, i have lacked the capacity to
make a choice or firmly claim a stance.

such a confident person who is so unconfident
in their own train of thought. conjuring
constant hypotheticals without managing to
make peace or deal with them accordingly.

i never really knew how to explain the inexplicable.

my crude father tried to help
make sense of what felt senseless by bluntly blurting out
a russian proverb:
"if grandma had balls, she'd be grandpa!"

*—trapped in a world of what-ifs*

growing up poor
does not necessarily mean
impoverished.

in my case,
it started off as assertation
that middle class lacks the means.

until one day,
the *dictator*
took everything from us,
in the midst
of my father's divorce
& changed my astute observations
entirely.

finances dwindled,
uneasiness set in.

there we were,
wondering if we could afford
our next meal or utilities for the month
& planning for the inevitable day
when someone would take
my childhood home
from us.

but we made the most of it
& did not let the means supersede
our yearning for a better tomorrow.

as we struggled,
my father reminded me that
you can make your dreams a reality
nothing is unattainable.

fruitful endeavors
are always within reach
if you know where to look.

i vowed to establish a strong work ethic
so that i would want for naught.

overworked and seemingly undereducated,
my obstacles soon turned to stepping stones.

i learned to enjoy life's spoils
to buy what i want
without remorse.

after all, you do not get to live twice.

classless societies are wonderful in sentiment but almost
impossible in practice.

i was fortunate enough to be given riches:
my father's love.

it kept life full of splendor and opportunity
in my eyes,
however, in our bank accounts...
poverty-stricken
didn't even begin to describe it.

always trying to make sense of dollars
without making dollars turn to cents.

years have gone by
& credit scores aside,
we are affluent.

possessing an abundance of care.
i call that "family money,"
it's something that no debt collector
can ever take from us.

blood is thicker than water;
that's true.

but the connection we shared was so meaningful that it
couldn't even be measured by volume.

moments shared were
so intimate and
conversations so purposeful
that they turned me into
the woman i am today; the woman i saw in you.

bonded by something deeper than a familial tie
brought together by choice.

grown,
nurtured,
& built to be the best i can be
all thanks to you, michelle.

forever grateful that you made
a daughter out of me.

to the woman who took me in
when no one else wanted me:

thank you for your sacrifices
& your fun-loving personality.

thank you for rescuing me
from my biological momster

& for teaching me
the important things
you felt i should know.

i'm so sorry
i never got the chance to give you
even half of what you gave me
before you passed.

i have deemed myself lucky
to have known you.
i feel like a child saying this,
but i need you.
i love you
effortlessly and endlessly,

& i will always miss my mommy.

i have been longing to bake you from scratch, crafted by
nature with my love.

my individual creation that gives me purpose,
i would nurture you to no end.

produced from the cells of our being.
i want to bask in love and reciprocity.

a mirror that loves me
just as much as i love it.

*—next concept(ion)*

sometimes my life feels like it's over,
like there's nothing left to do.

my life could be over
i've even wished it too.

then i consider
a new chance at life.
a chance just for you.

the life i give you
will be of the utmost importance;
i swear to you.

there's so much you've yet to do.
baby of mine,
life has been hard
& may continue to be;

just remember,
you were conceived
through heartbreak
then gave life back to me.

you are made of magic,
my only glimmer of hope,
the one that keeps me going.

my bleak existence feels brighter
as my mind revolves around
thoughts of who you could be.

if the day does come
& my dream comes true,
my child,
you'll achieve such greatness;
i will it for you.

*—first born*

this is my life:

painful
rugged
full of adoration after
my experiences
& oh-so-many mistakes.

so many i miss
so many i have loved,
lost,
& let go...

yet somehow,
i find myself
weeping out of utter joy.

for those who have made
an impression on me,
i'm ever so grateful.

you're the reason why
i am still standing
after all these years.
flawed,
learning,
desperately giving
& accepting of love.

so again, i say thank you for you,
& i love you
even when i hate you.

i overflow with appreciation
more than my breath can bear
to explain in an exhale.

thank you.

to the people who chose me,
who chose to stay,
who didn't help create
the severe abandonment issues that
plague my day to day.

thank you.

to all that wanted to
alleviate rather than
perpetuate the pain
in my relationships and my mind,
i will forever feel indebted to you
my only constants,
my greatest gifts.

thank you.

scar tissue stuck to the place where my heart should have been—papier-mâché.

hand-me-downs given as secondhand care—tattered.

lack of attention seeping into my lonesome subconscious—neglect.

constantly questioning intentions of people who have been cared for—curiosity.

taking note of the void where my connections should be—awareness.

somehow, lack of love from others taught me to love myself—acceptance & growth.

*—adolescent lessons*

beauty can bloom
in the darkest of places.
therein lies the inner workings
of trauma.

the mistakes i've made
have been carefully placed in
the emotional baggage i carry
as i move through life.

i don't know how i'm able to
bring it out in public anymore.
not many notice it,
but i always know it's there—
worn down and full of despair.
with each day,
it feels as if it is too heavy to bear.

i am haunted by this,
but the bag will never tear.
it is in each stage of consciousness
& it plagues me, i swear.
this feels like a never-ending nightmare.

no matter how hard i try
to forget it
to leave it somewhere
my mental manages to remind me
to bring it along.

i am ashamed and regretful,
but there's nothing i can do
so i share it with you
& pray that one day
it is taken off my shoulders, too.

i am so tired
but i wouldn't dare
let anyone hold it for me.
it is too ugly and has a knack for
making life feel unfair.

so i walk with this bag
an heirloom of sorts.

i wait for the day when i am buried,
& we can both be spared
by being put to rest.

but for the time being, we remain
in this limbo that lacks luster.

surviving, not thriving.

as i walk through my life's experiences with you,
it may feel as though you're taking a walk
in my tattered old shoes.

you will see the paths i've traveled
how i've gone the wrong way
then had to turn myself around.

disclaimer: i have gotten lost a time or ten.

but somehow, i always manage to
get where i intended to go.

now, i stand here in the past for a moment—
only to bask in how wonderfully fleeting
it all was.

knowing it's is over is seemingly pleasant.
now, i see how much time i spent mulling over
such trivial matters,
such surface-level emotions.

so marvelously unimportant.

putting pen to paper
helped me understand my pain,
& yet my pain is what made me
put pen to paper.

an unwelcomed visitor takes it upon themself to come
into my life unannounced and follow me everywhere i go.

posing as a distraction and decreasing my
effectiveness by plaguing me with pain monthly.

crying
screaming
aching

i beg and plead; i say, "please leave," to no avail.

when i am finally alone once more, relief is
overshadowed by a realistic fear: this time is limited.

my visitor will always be near;
after all, it lives within me.

see you next month, endometriosis.

chronic pain is scarier than murder.
not a matter of if
but a matter of when
it is unbearable to no foreseeable end.

it is a deep and dull suffering that
painkillers cannot even kill.

what hurts you doesn't make you stronger
in this instance. but it also won't kill you,
and that is arguably the worst part.

my surgical scars
some internal
are a story of survival
pain endured, attached to trials and tribulations
in untold sickness and in health.

there is no dignity in suffering,
though there is tolerance in existing.

there is not always strength in survival
especially when it is endured alone.

having illnesses that result in procedures
teaches you about what is important in life
what is most important to you,
for it is all relative.

even with the physical pain dispersed throughout my
body, somehow, i'm never distracted enough to dull the
feeling for you.

will you be at my bedside when i need you most?
will you be there when the anesthesia wears off?

the most dangerous path
is the one i followed
running into the chicago night
as if there's no tomorrow

i left the night crawling
i refused to let go
got sucked into the industry
a huge black hole

one venue after another
in a merry-go-round of
detrimental drugs,
meaningless sex,
& cdjs.

soul sucking bottom feeders
depleted my aura
until i was merely a reflection of them.

"friends"
entered and exited my life
just the same.

i became part of the "in crowd"
a local celebrity
the ultimate status symbol
what a meaningless prize
the ultimate distraction
in a hollow place

are the familiar faces
really that familiar?

how do they "know me"
if i still don't know them?

how do they recognize me
when i no longer recognize myself?

cheating,
lying,
& scheming
to the beat of the bass.

late nights
turned to
murky mornings
it was all so hazy

an unsustainable life.

how does one crawl out of this rut?
keep going until you see the light
near the exit of the venue.

my parting gift?
my dignity.

retelling stories from the past
has become a common feat.

each time, it's met with criticism
over moments that have become obsolete.

the memories of which we speak
feel as though they are from a lifetime ago,
a reality i no longer know.

the good news is
i'm pretty much who i say i am.

the bad news is
i'm pretty much who i say i am.

learning and living my life
while shamelessly and unforgivably
in my element.

—*unbothered*

my familial roots
are so deeply embedded
that they've become
my sense of security.

feet so firmly planted on the ground
that i am afraid to move.

although, i don't think
i'll ever be comfortable enough
to stay away...

i also realize that the art of exploring
is the best way to encounter experiences
within other spaces in different places
with their own unique tastes and traditions.

where i reside, i am comfortably stuck, and you may be
too. still, i implore you to travel and learn some things you
never knew.

but don't forget where you came from just yet
because home will always be a place that's
waiting for you.

coming and going as i please:
41° 9773° n, 87° 8369° w.

loving and learning while traveling.

however, i cannot seem to learn to love the vessel
that carries me from point a to point b.

83 ft is all it takes for me to fill with regret and completely
forget why i chose to endure this in the first place.

still, i find myself constantly craving more. needing new
experiences and ultimately fighting fear to see the world.

*—planes*

where do we go from here?
what's next?

*—a new*

love

my favorite love story
is the one we wrote together
the one i made with you.

a lot of this is for a gentleman i once knew,
& i'm hoping that
he finally knows
my words are true.

*—an ode to you*

my love language is eloquence.

—*diction*

his lips were quicksand

the more he spoke,
the more i felt his lips on mine,
the more i sunk into him...

i love the way you think
listening to you speak
makes me turn pink

your shaggy long brown hair
oh god the way you stare

that dimple in your cheek
you make me so damn weak

the cutest boy i swear
i feel so unprepared

when our eyes finally link
you always give a wink

it's more than i can bear
guess love is in the air.

we are always on the
same wavelength
in different bodies of water

& yet,
i still manage to
drown in you.

i want to embrace you tenderly,

caress you,

& feel your breath
on the nape of my neck
only for tonight.

my clothes will melt away
at the touch of your hands,

& i'll be yours for the taking
only for tonight.

call me baby

& feel the flirtation
only for tonight.

be one with my body
only for tonight.

forget about the consequences

& push regret aside
only for tonight.

don't be gentle while you play with me
only for tonight.

admire the decadence of
how lustfully sinful we behave
only for tonight.

taste me with intentions
to never forget me

even after tonight.

*—cravings*

she's growing to enjoy
the sensual lashings
her lover leaves her with

while also noticing
the resemblance to what she received
as a child.

*—regression bound by s&m*

i love you
for loving me
when i feel
unlovable.

your touch is my drug

& addiction always leads to instability...
even when i'm clean,

i still find myself
craving you, my vice.

*—passionately destructive*

even now,
the time we spent together
exudes through these pages.

every time you read my words,
i will come back to you.

*—muse*

i've got your body on my mind
so vivid and enthralling.

remembering all the ways
you've made music out of me
the sweetest release.

completely consuming as i let
your light enter the depths of my darkness.

exhaling euphorically
when your name trails off my breath.

goosebumps all over,
chills down my spine.

my body physically translates
the tension
& feels the satisfaction

of us,
on me,
on you.

over and over
in my head.

*—climax*

when in passionate relationships,
it is easy for logic to go out the window

acting on emotions
catapulting into the unknown
without contemplating
the consequences,
living in love.

if you are thinking logically,
that says enough about how you feel.

i have always been bad at directions,
so here i stand yet again,
permanently lost in love.

*—hopeless romantic*

you're my north star.

where you go,
i follow without question.

i always know that
i'm going the right way
when that route leads me to you.

can love define us if we struggle to define love?

i had love
& then love had me.

i am bound to you,
& you belong to me.

—codependency

i can't have you halfway, baby;
can't even try.

i just love you so much, sugar;
will you be mine?

i can't wait around to
find out what may be, my dearest,
for you are all there is
to me.

tell me what you want, lover;
won't you stop toying with me...

i'll give you what you need, sweetie;
you don't even have to say please.

no time to sit back and live in the moment;
can't you see that
your indecisiveness
is hurting me.

so, make up your mind, honey,
please hold true.
be sure to end up with me, darling;
i beg of you.

stay with me, handsome;
i plead.

stay for me, sexy;
i'll even get on my knees.

stay with me, angel,
for i will open up to you and
finally let you see
all that there is to me.

just don't you leave.

even when you are not confident in me,
just know i am devoted to you.

you are my for better or for worse
you can be better, and i can be worse
as long as i get to be with you.

i will never be poor
if i am able to indulge
in the richness of
our time spent together.

i will carry the burden of sickness
for your health.

i will love you deeply
while
i cherish you constantly.

even in death,
we will never part.

—*my vow*

not sure what's better,
but late isn't never.

you now have
this part of us
forever.

i now understand why it is called "falling in love."

the same fall cannot happen twice.
even though we are able to fall
over and over again.

sometimes landing without a scratch,
others badly bruised,
some, worst of all,
without the potential of revival.

we can't control the momentum at which it happens,
and the landing is dependent upon
displacing the energy of the body.

then we plummet:
hearts racing,
minds pacing,
enveloped in earth-shattering love.

*—free fall*

♡

your life makes me happy;
i hope you love to live it.

you don't have to drop the world for me.
my moments with you mean the world.

you always loved water.
fluidity was your self-expression,

you were always able to run with the tides
while simultaneously
pulling me in deeper.

even when we sank,
i never felt like
i needed to come up for air.

you were the sea,
so much greater than me,
& i was fortunate to have been able to swim within the
depths of you.

we come back to each other in waves;
i will forever be standing by the shore

waiting for the next storm to come
wishing i could swim again.

i have faith that you're worth having faith in.

sayings vs reality:

how can i continue to be the "cool girl"
when my body emits heat every time you're around?

how can i take things "day by day"
when i desperately want you
to be my, day to day?

"life goes on,"
how am i supposed to go on
when you only live on
in my dreams?

if i only "want what i can't have,"
then it is clear that i have only been given
what i do not want.

relationships are not always amorous.

sometimes the love potion doesn't mix properly,
instead, it creates a poison that will only lead to emotional
demise.

is the toxic symbol legible?
depends how quickly you move it
to proceed without caution...

*—learning to read signs*

i destroy you
just to overindulge in you
once more.

then catch you going through my shit
& push you away
just to drag you back
through my mess
then talk you up
until you feel blessed.

still your suspicions linger
then they trigger freak-outs
encased in doubt.

potential obstacles are planted
in your mind
until we become
fated to repeat them.

each having said too much
to ever take it back.

a stint in a prison that is served voluntarily.

trust is broken,
lies are spoken,
making us overdose
on the bad
& hazily forget the good.

lovers so scorned.

despite it all,
the fiend still craves
their addiction

pleasure
& pain.

i am that disease;
the pill
you just can't help
but swallow.

*—your kim*

the greatest disguise is the one you wear
when you look me in the eyes and tell me
there's no love there.

i know you pine,
& i do too.

this little spiel you've made up
is just not true.

i must confess,
i see right through you.

the biggest player
has turned into
a hopeless romantic

wishing for endless options with you...
do you feel it too?

because it's beginning to seem
as though i will only be friends with you.

i don't want to admit it,
though we both know

to wish for something that won't come true
is not the smartest choice,

but still i do.

you may seem hard to love
to the people who don't deserve you

& here i sit jealously
watching
from an outsider's point of view.

understanding each intention
while crying out
hoping you'll realize
this is not what's fated
for us.

the changes made
for our love's gain
is something
i took too long to claim.

i should have only had eyes
for you.
for now, i do,

& time's run out.

*—more than acquaintances, less than lovers*

i can't live in a state of
"we will see"
with you
because
all i see is you.

i look for you in every crowd
i see you when you're not around.

on the streets where we once walked
in all the spaces we had talked

although you're never there
i still can't help but stare

even when you're not around
i somehow keep you safe and sound.

# loss

i have spent my life
watching the people who surround me
leave.

now, i help them pack
as i push them further away
& embrace them intensely
as i hug them goodbye.

only to then grieve their loss...

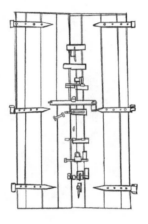

—*my reckoning*

old friends will always have a seat at my table
even if they choose to leave it empty.

*—newfound strangers*

my first forever
was what i had always thought of you
although these days,
"friends forever"
doesn't quite ring true.

as time goes on,
we must follow
down separate paths
leading us to a new tomorrow.

that next day
that once felt so far away
is sorrowful and blue.

all emotions
due to knowing that
there is no longer me and you.

the greatest bond
has now been broken,
& there are no words
left to be spoken.

*—falling out*

what once brought us together
is now tearing us apart.

so, how do we adapt to the loss?

*—growing pains*

a friendship lost
does not necessarily equate
to a foe gained.

—*unrequited*

all the words we left unsaid
keep running through my head.

the silence reverberates
throughout my mind.

it jolts me to my core
each and every time.

here i am, stuck in this state of *mine*.

my sorrow spilled over into a realization:

i didn't truly know what "*i miss you*" meant
until i reached for your hand and you were no longer
there.

—*longing*

i miss you
even though i've never met you.

& i loved you,
even while circumstances
kept us apart.

it seems as though
you were never mine to have.

*—abortion*

my sorrowed sobs felt trivial
within the torrential downpour.

*—bigger than me*

riding can be so free yet so final.

a cruise can be turned into an abrupt destination.

a distance driven that can be measured by insurmountable loss.

a grief so intense that it can only be felt as fear.

the ultimate anguish.

a world, our existence came crashing down around me the moment that motorcycle did.

*—r.i.p. mom*

trying to tear myself away
from tangible things
that make me think of you.

*—nonmaterialistic*

separation anxiety can be debilitating.
when every fiber of your being
hopes they'll stay
knowing
there is nothing you can do about it.

becoming aware of this notion is crippling,
attempting to move forward
without moving on,
coming to terms with missing
the most important part of yourself.

moments lessen
miles expand
in memories as well as physical distance,
thus, leaving only a mirage
of what used to be.

some of the most difficult
losses are comprised of the living.

they are not gone and they are
most certainly not forgotten.

there is nothing besides your mental
to be put to rest
no cemetery to visit
to feel as though they're near you
in order to decompress.

they simply live in
a world that no longer involves you.

& the pain of being bid adieu
is arguably more painful
than the death of you.

*—heart transplant*

as my tears hit the paper
& my breathing quickens

i'm left feeling like my blood thickens,
while all i can think of is you.

i remember you.

do you remember me too?

*—gone but never forgotten*

to the *lost ones*
who once lived among us:

it must've been hard for you
to make sense of what felt senseless.

responsibilities were too heavy to hold;
when you fell, i fell with you.

knowing that you will no longer be
has sent me down a spiral of sadness;
did you think of me?

i can't imagine
how hard it must've been for you;
did you get a chance to look out for you?

when this happened to you,
it happened to me too.

what are we to do
now that you have ended you?

i am sorry that you felt
there was nothing else to do.
now, i can't bear to have lost you.

you were never alone.
so many souls have
suffered and settled it with suicide...

*—i forgive you*

looking back on us,
our sentiments seem to be so similar
yet just far enough out of reach,
to feel as though they can be questioned.

the connections and obstacles
shared between us were a hamster wheel neither
of us ever took the time to get off of.

such intellectual people,
so shamefully detrimental
to their own happiness
when given something profound

always daylight savings time.
nobody knows why, even so,
they play along and self-sabotage.

the most permanent version of
the beginning of the end.

a tragic loss story
tied together with love
that's always found.

the original inevitable cliff-hanger.

i'm a little late
& you're a little early,
which makes me walk frantically

trying to find a route
that will make us
meet in the middle.

*—timing is everything*

i was always halfway out the door
waiting for my lover
to pull me back in.

then when i got used to you,
you got rid of me;
now, how am i expected to be?

ruminating over my past
while completely overlooking my present
as i crave your presence.

holding on to pieces of a puzzle
that had already been taken apart,
diving deeper into delusion
as i wait for you.

i wish i knew that
the little things were the big things
when i had them.

i should never have granted my mind
the ability to take you for granted.

praying that if i pressed re-start
it would actually turn out positive.

although, i do not only
have myself to blame,
maybe you just
didn't feel the same.

if you did,
then you must've missed
that special something in me.

i guess that you just didn't see.
maybe it was hidden,
or maybe it just recently came to be.

it's a shame that you were blinded
to all these feelings
i felt for thee.

you deserve the love i didn't know how to give you.

—*i miss you*

the way you used to
hold me when we slept,
now, keeps me up at night.

my long-lost lover
comes back to me
in melodies of music
with stories untold.

*—severed ties*

my dreams now
feel like nightmares.
because they're so pleasant
i see you so vividly that
i could almost feel you.

then you are ripped away
as soon as i open my eyes.

your name is the first thing
my conscious mind registers,
my own personal morning sickness.

xanax can't even calm the crying
when reality wakes.

still, i sing myself lullabies;
eagerly in anticipation
i cannot wait to go back to sleep each night
in hopes of being close to a fictitious you.

because i've felt numb
since the last time that
i was actually able to be with you
in a world that wasn't
r.e.m.

the only reality i want
is the one with you in it...

part of me died
& is living inside of someone else.

*—i gave you my heart*

i feel the safest when i lie to myself
until i feel fully convinced enough
to say that:

"one day, you'll love me again.
you'll actually come back
& whisk me away."

*—(false) hope*

i keep going through the motions
but how do i motion back to you?

pieces of you
still fill my place,
even without you
in my space.

you see,
i wanted to be in it with you
for the long haul,
but i couldn't get past
your wall.

now i'm getting to a point
where i need to set boundaries
to my heart's divide.

i cannot continue to
fantasize about
a life you will not provide.

it all has felt too real,
all in all, i'm just trying to heal...

fully succumbing to each other
destroyed us mentally
even before the breakup.

amidst our own insanity,
we became bad in what felt like
someone else's story.

now, looking back at the ruins
can be quite rough,
then, i think to myself:

*damn we had fun, didn't we?*

how do i constantly miss what we could've
had if we never had it in the first place?

our relationship was destined for disaster.

somehow, we managed to crash
without collision.

so unstable,
an immense ticking time bomb
that came at the utmost cost;

what made me flatline was that i felt i had lost.

i had fought for you for so long
i even went to war with myself
which proved to be fatal.

while you made it out seemingly unscathed.

we reap what we sow,
& it has made us so grim.

therefore, i have come to see
that my toxic trait
is loving you before me.

it's like after the war;
when you rip off the
blood-soaked gauze
& treat the wound
to no avail,

breakups
can make you feel like
a wounded soldier.

there is now
an indication that you have to
sever the entire limb.
your limb.

to cut off the dead weight
that stopped
working for you.

*—phantom heart*

i thought my grand finale
would've been with you,
however, that has proven to be untrue.

living in the same household
might as well be eons apart,

so, what will be
will be
& with our mutual contempt
i am starting to feel as though that
does not end with us as a "we."

i fear that
we may tear each other apart
for we were not meant for each other
from the start.

so please tell me,
what are we supposed to do?
now that i've completely
fallen out of love with you?

& honestly, if i were you,
i would probably leave me too.

if the loss is so heavy,
then how can you ever truly feel
what you may gain after the fact?

benevolence
holds no relevance
in the midst of dismay.

how can it be their loss if it gravely feels like it's mine?

the misfortunate moments come with comprehension

for it is not my loss,
nor is it theirs.

it is ours.

in order to learn to live
without you,
i will have to unlearn everything
i thought i knew.

*—i carry you with me*

i made a mistake and left the man i loved
replaced "us" with
a replica relationship
swore that it felt right
but i was wrong
believed i found something just as good
but i completely misunderstood
it's not where i was supposed to be at all.
& i have never felt so small.
i don't have the answers.
it's like every time i choose
i lose.

*—a modern-day calamity*

you have become so mentally
ingrained in my brain that
even when i'm with him,
i feel you.

-*fantasize*

you were supposed to be my forever,
but that ended.

& yet i still haven't run out of time...

i've forgiven you by finally forgiving myself.

—*we are going to be alright*

i hope you're happy
but
not happier than you were with me
& that's the best version
of my blessing
that there could possibly be.

yeah, maybe that seems selfish
but i just can't
fucking help it.

i want the best for you
but the best
that you can do
is the version of myself
that i am learning to be
just you wait and see

but if you want someone
other than me
then that's just what it'll be.

i hope you're happy
but please
don't be happier than you were with me
i sorta feel sorry for them
for you
cause they will never know you
the way that i do
that much is simply true.

you may even start to love another
but
i sorta feel sorry for them
for you
cause that love will pale in comparison
to what i had with you.

still, i hope you have a
happily ever after,
i really do
but please just don't be happier

long a little longer
don't be happier
than you were
with me.

you said you had a type:
it was me.

then you "moved on" and somehow always found a girl
who looked the part.

these carbon copies measured in quantity with a lack of
quality.

they will never be me.

honey, don't you see, that in this case
imitation is not
the sincerest form
of flattery.

*—close but not quite*

you circled around me
through mutual acquaintances
but always remained out of reach.

i was forced by your hand
to walk through life alone
no matter how much i pleaded for an alternative.

i had to attempt to come to terms with
living at arm's length from you,
but there you were,
constantly peering meticulously from afar
while critiquing my motions without ever allowing me to
hear your thoughts.

days turned into months,
& you began to feel like a mirage.
that's when i realized
you would only meet me at my level
when the light left my eyes.

—vulture

when i wrote this
i thought it was for you
the boy from
my past
with whom i thought love would surely last.
see, i know we weren't perfect
but you still made me feel
like you were worth it

you've always been my muse
constantly in my mind
you were there to use.

i tried to win you back
i gave it my best
& this book was my plan of attack

words loaded
heart exploded
awaiting your review

now it is out
& there is still
no trace
of you

so
maybe it was all a test...
if that's the case, i'm not impressed
your indifference proves that we are through
& there is nothing left for me to do.

spelling all of this out was a gesture
i knew i'd never be able to undo
& then i guess i sorta left it up to you

did you know?
could you tell?
if so,
then
what the fuck
did you plan
to do?

wouldn't meet me halfway
guess it was too much to ask
left with no expectations
honestly,
thought i'd be broken but that is untrue
i'm actually grateful that i was so open
'cause now there are no words left unspoken.

it was our chance
the last possible thing i could do
for romance

clearly
it didn't work
& honestly
i think you're a fucking jerk

nonetheless,
this is my mess
to that i can attest.

guess the point of you
was only
art

i feel like an idiot
for trying to make you
acknowledge
my heart

i can no longer play this game
so i will attempt to forget your name
while pondering
whether or not
we have each other to blame

the boy from my past
with whom love was never meant
to last.

sometimes the most
memorable response
is no response at all.

*—your silence is deafening*

i live my life on your terms
feeling like an option really fucking burns.

so, i try to pull you back
but my closeness only extends
as far as your distance allows.

i keep telling myself that
i am only reaching out to you for "closure"
though we both know
it's been done,
it's over.

*—unjust justifications*

lamenting my woes within the prose.

i must confess;
i feel that all this loss needs to be put to rest.
it tends to make me feel hopeless,
& then i'm left with nothing to cope with...

i cannot withstand holding onto this mess
my hands are hot
my head is heavy
so i am trying
to transfer the weight
from parts of me
onto these pieces of paper.

praying that
the end of this book
is also the end of us,
of this.

i don't know how much longer
i can grieve over it all.

therefore, i am writing
purging on paper
& leaving it up to you,
dear reader.

i am no longer
in the condition
to feel
to do.

the life i start to live
by myself
for myself
must commence.

# & the infinite aftermath

my life experiences
taught me to love
& dealt me plenty of loss
that inevitably lead up
to the infinite aftermath.

how can i plan for the future
& be in the present
when i so deeply miss my past?

*—life's labyrinth*

fair warning:

this may be an utter mess
of overexpression,

i digress...

sometimes i'm alone
& do not feel lonely

but often
i feel lonely when
i am not
alone.

*—balancing act*

outward:
people are neither good nor are they bad;
it's just life
& the role they play in yours
makes you believe them to be
one or the other.

meanwhile

inward:
each of us draws an inherent level of
conflict upon ourselves
& fails to adequately see our role
in the situation until
we're looking back at it.

*—life's looking glass*

what i've come to understand is that
i have so much to learn
so much knowledge i'm eager to obtain

& yet i am constantly asking questions
i don't want the answers to.

intricately complicated.

beautifully tragic.

calmly chaotic.

irrationally argumentative.

deeply demanding.

debilitatingly depressed.

but still so sexy even while sad.

*—an aura*

you are a work of art
always worth at least a glance.

everyone has a different perspective
of your meaning.

those who are an admirer of yours have an appreciation
for the refined.

*—the finest of arts*

a lesson to be learned:

the hand is a very interesting thing...

why?

because it closes toward you;
no matter which way you try to bend it
or how you try to ignore it,
it still folds inward.

meaning:
people are selfish by nature;
it's in their physicality.

the act of doing for others
is a conscious decision
to move past nature
& attempt nurture.

can't help feeling like
we are in constant limbo
where time is of the essence
& yet it is constantly wasted.

*—living in little moments*

become so comfortable with
your own reflection
that nobody can ever convince you
that you are anything
other than you.

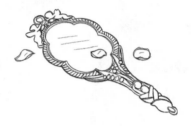

where i am is not where i want to be,
but how i get there is up to me.

even so, it does show that
i am not who i was,
& that's so good for me;
for i am working to be
a better me.

i'm rude when i am in a mood
whimsically witty with my loved ones.
i cope with things by making them apparent and then
laughing at my own pain.
i set high expectations, and some call me vain,
but i am not appalled
at their disdain.

my mischievous movements
often turn to
mundane moments
that leave me in
melancholy moods,

but i live and i learn while constantly reevaluating
ruminating
what was i doing?
did it have to be done for me to become the woman i am?
i guess that's up to me.
so, who are you to speak of me?

—*my prerogative*

quit concerning yourself
with things that
do not concern you.

the only business
that should be minded
is your own.

i am
a walking talking oxymoron
the master of my own success
& demise.

*—contradictions*

i am controlling of others
because i have no self-control.

what you see is what you get:
my subconscious is a picture book
full of illustrations—recollections strewn throughout
pages.

flowing in & out of my mind
like waves of communication;
traveling through time
reveling in what's done
but
not forgotten.

thoughts
creatively curated
but never constant
become memories placed on pieces of paper
meticulously measured
throughout
moments in time.
even some that rhyme.

now, let's tell the truth:
i'm so fucking insecure
when i think about some of these things,
i feel so fucking immature.
writing down words
i didn't even know i meant
how could i,
when all my time was spent
pretending that none of this was ever even felt.

my mind is
screaming
my heart is
bleeding

my world ends where this book begins
it intrudes and exudes
past the means of my moods.

outward and upward into the universe
way past the stars
painting the sky
with all of my scars.

some tattoos are internal.

i've come to learn that
you have to choose
to be aware of your own issues
because nobody is going to
solve them for you

& unfortunately,
they will not magically solve themselves.

if you don't, then chaos and toxicity
ensues in behavior and relationships

these are hard lessons
taught by harder obstacles.
so, you must become self-aware
in order to stand your ground.

my brain is at max capacity
producing and inducing
anxiety.

what is going on up there?
why is it all such a mess?
will it ever let me be?

it shouldn't be this difficult;
do others have it as hard as me?

mistakes cut deep into a heavy head,
the pain seeps down into the soul and out through the
slits in the wrists.

*—bleeding heart*

hating yourself
is the worst type of violence,
a war within the mind.

trenches,
emotional bombs detonating,
a fight with constant casualties
& ultimate survival
without reward.

the epitome of eternal damnation.

a purple heart is known to be one of valor
however, it can also be one that is bruised.

they cannot make you
bend to their will and agree
unless you want to.

part of being an independent adult
is being able to make choices on your own;
be happy with them.

if you regret something,
that is solely for you to say—nobody else.

life is full of mixed reviews.
that's why opinions exist,
& we are all entitled to our own.

i have seen flowers bloom
from the dirtiest depths of the earth's soil,

& you,
my darling,
have sprouted.
your ground-shattering petals have been displayed
for the world to see.

*—metamorphosis*

don't you see, sweetie,
you've survived
through all the love and pain,
the loss and gain.

traveled through
your own infinite aftermath
& look at how far you came.

even when it felt like
you wouldn't
or absolutely couldn't,
you rose from your own hellfire.

you may wonder
how i could possibly know this
it simply couldn't be true,

but you are here
reading the words i've written.
a tale of surviving,
written for the survivor
by a survivor.

it's okay to not want to stay
until last call
but, honey, please try.

missing an opportunity
leaves you with opportune time
to catch the next one;
don't give up just yet.

you can be a queen on a chessboard
as long as you strategically
set your sights on something
& move accordingly.

the power you yield
is encased in your choices.
they set up the future for you.

now, make sure you ensure that
it's a victory.

*—no knights needed*

you are allowed to make a big deal
out of things that are a big deal to you.

no need to be soft spoken
because they matter
oh yes, they do.

a *plethora* of mercurial *men* have created my mood *swings*.

—*pms*

drama always seems to find me.

theatrics fill my headspace and bring out the performance of a lifetime.

staying calm is not an option when the lines roll off the tongue and the emotion pours out onto the crowd.

acting out and surprising the audience as well as the cast members until the final scene.

a hush is casted, and it becomes ever so evident that the end of the show is not necessarily the end of the world.

take it from a drama pro: sometimes in the most unforeseeable moments, someone will find meaning in your role and give you a standing ovation.

—*curtain call*

can you learn from your mistakes while simultaneously repeating them?

*—foolish wisdom*

the way promiscuity drips from me
like honey-coated
sweetened dreams
is not what you may think it to be,

for i am just a pawn
in the portion of my brain
that urges me to do
so much wrong.

in these sugarcoated scenes
i am unaware
although
it seems that i want to do
all that i say i do;

i make the impulsive choice
to open myself up
to you.

while you attempt to pull
the liquor from my lips
& grab me by my throat and hips
you hear me tease
& sometimes even watch me
drip and please

all in all,
this is my manic pitfall.

yeah, it was hot,
i felt it too

the way i toyed around with you

with every
mouthwatering craze
& scandalous embrace
you must know

that i would take it all back
for a mundane rapport
that i never knew i craved
until
i realized that the most delicious taste
is a lick
of self-control.

boundaries are a mentally stable person's safety net.

—*lessons i lacked*

how can i have respect for you
if i don't have it for myself?

*—first things first*

am i dead inside?

detached
introverted
socially sociopathic
stoic

just, me.

*—unfazed*

does making it through the day
in a mediocre way
make you feel okay?

can you hear it?
the sound of static
stagnant
aren't you
sick because you've settled?

silence swept over you
indicating indifference.

finally understanding
why your friends tried to meddle
knowing that there is nothing you can say
if you stay
because it will always remain this way

what will it take?
for you to finally
let go?

don't you see?
all this time you thought this was
a team of two
turns out, it was only you
doing better
by yourself, for yourself.

—*it's settled, don't settle*

to miss what was unhealthy is natural,
but to retreat and fall back
into that painful pattern is
a disservice to
yourself.

choose to do better and be better,
for the version of you
that is sitting on the other side
of this terrible time.

people try to placate
they say that it is okay not to be okay
well guess what?
it doesn't feel that way.

probably because
it's not.

that is life:
making what you can
out of what you cannot
change.

you are not a failure, my darling...

you just fail to pay attention
to the things that are important.

focus on the betterment of you,
& everything else will start to align.

*—trust me*

getting burned is inevitable.
you'll feel the pain,
the singe.

it'll change you,
but you have the option
to choose how.

you can either live in avoidance
as to not obtain another scar
you'll undoubtedly have to peel back and eventually
reference

or you can take the pain and
turn it into pleasure

learn to spit fire
& create tricks that
people will applaud you for.

—options

being crazy is a new millennial artistry.

—*antipsychotics sold separately*

opinions unveiled are
hard pills to swallow.

as if i don't already
have enough of them
to consume from
my psychiatrist.

—rx

how thin is the line between
substance use and substance abuse?

will a blackout help you find out?

is that something you'd still like to do
even if it subsequently ruins you?

dear male caller,

i trusted you for years,
yet somehow
you took advantage of me.

you trespassed the barrier of my mind,
then entered my body without a "yes, please."

a mind you cannot exit.
a body you betrayed.

you left me
tainted and untrusting.
i don't recall asking for it.

society told me
i was supposed to respect you...
if only they knew
how you broke me.

—rape

the semicolon i wear
is a subtle reminder to pause—
for a moment.

it's not an ending
rather a continuance...
telling me to appreciate what's before me,
both literally and metaphysically.

i speak on this with hesitation
as i remind myself there was
a time,
a single thought,
where i found myself
debating on
or facilitating
an end.

playfully dancing with death...

always pulling back
towards life.

this pause of a semicolon
poses a problem because
it cannot definitively be looked back on
as the past.

it is a continuance—
an attempt, even,
to try to change,
& to simply be.

time spent,
scars left,
tears wept.

then the dialogue continues
where we left off,
without pause
to no end.

i quizzically ponder to myself:

was i meant to be this unhappy?
is this the only way that art,
would burst from my heart?
if not, then where the fuck would i start?

i will never know
so, as the tears start to flow,
i pick up my pen and paint the picture of
my pain
still feeling like it's all in vain.

even when i'm stark sober
the depression never seems to be over
maybe it's some kind of lesson
all in all, i can't stop stressin'
this feeling has become innate

at times i wonder
if i am what i create and if that is the case,
then why does my creation
fill me with such hate?

have i lost my mind, or am i just lost in my mind?

manic mornings
turn to
nocturnal nights
at the slowest quickening pace.

neurotic euphoria is fixated upon
without the slightest notion.

my alternate universe
trickles over
into your reality.

*—improperly medicated*

how are you supposed to understand me if i barely understand myself?

my disorder does not define me.

yet i am constantly defining myself
within the parameters of my disorder.

—*bipolar*

i wish i meant it when i say
i don't give a damn,
but that is just not who i really am.

when my tongue has time to rattle my mind
the concrete walls i built suddenly crack
then my saliva leaks and spews awful things
as i unravel at the seams.

always a spiral set off that rivals a tornado.

i tear down your stable structure
with gusts of wind that burst from whatever
my mouth can muster.

i scream so loud
i move with such violence that
wreckage piles up and doomsday
lives on until
damage is surely done.

& so, you will wonder how a little girl
who is 5'2 that "never cares"
felt so deeply that she did all she could do
to make herself big enough
to destroy parts of you.

*—i am a natural disaster*

*please start* to pay *attention:*

what if you take your time
& then time runs out?

life will live on
even if you are not lively.

it will slip by,
& you will be left
wondering how it happened.

feeling like another lifetime,
another reality,
a different you.

*—psa*

throughout my life,
i have always felt like
i was treading water
in between two boats

looking back longingly
at the one that has passed
while wondering why i let it go

if i should have,
could have,
would have.

while simultaneously awaiting
the approaching boat
with eager anticipation.

skittishly looking at both options.

which boat is the one i need?
can i trust myself to make the right choice?

the answer is quite simple
neither.

being self-sufficient enough to
build my own boat
is the best thing
i could possibly do.
to set off sailing
calmly and confidently.

mood and mind as deep as can be.

the older we get, the less shallow we seem.
all becomes so clear.

bask in the light, sunshine.
soak it all up.

then when ready and rested,
go toward the shade to relax and reflect
because that is the best
a mental vacation can get.

to all the books i have read:

thank you for entering my life and library
i have fallen in love with your words.

ink on a body
is pleasant to the eyes.

while

ink on a novel
is soothing for the soul.

*—permanence*

a woman of routine,
a creature of habit.

& yet
there is something
so admirable about
the consistently

inconsistent.

*—organized chaos*

no one wants to hear me talk
princess pessimistic
morbid little mistress
honey, did you miss it?

probably just dismissed it
oh well, i'll start to ramble
just to see what you can handle
i scream cause i have
my
bad days
bad dreams
bad years
& dirty little fears.

oh now
you're all ears?

then welcome to the shit show baby
we can drive each other crazy
i'll be with you
but i'll miss me
as soon as you are around
to kiss me.

you know i'm
never happy
always sappy
things are crappy

are you sick of me yet?
oh, baby, i'll bet.

my glass seems to be
half empty

but somehow
i always find myself
swallowing a mouthful.

                    *—the human condition*

to my critics
in life and in literature:

thank you for taking the time
to read with me.

i'm sure you see;
life is not necessarily
my cup of tea.

so, while i drink my coffee,
i will set aside my delusions
& let you come to
your own conclusions.

i love the criticism
so, don't you fret,
you do not offend me.

stained and impure.
we are not the same.
for this is a novel, and you are _____.

*—i am not for everyone*

all i have is myself
at the end of the day
& i want that to be okay

for some reason,
i never feel as though i'm enough
even though people
are constantly telling me
that i'm too damn much.

all i have is myself
at the end of the day
still, i have so much left to prove

head heavy with
self-doubt
self-pity
self-loathing
these things are found within me

at the end of the day
all i have is
myself.

so i ask,
how do i teach myself to be okay?

with only
me.
myself
& i.

i hope these chaotic words that
never helped me,
somehow bring
peace and healing
unto you, dear reader.

my work is done;
& if you are reading
in search of connection,
that means neither you nor i
are alone.

# about the book

rly's rousing prose and poetry collection fill the soul and mind with an everlasting longing for life.

made through magdalena godlewska's looking glass; complete with cover art by eva evangelista and illustrations by sarah emig.

# about the author

rly is a russian american writer and poet raised in the chicago-land area, making her dream come true with the creation of this novel.

for her, writing is the most riveting release. books provide her peace and comfort when all else seems to waver.

@prosebyrly